The Clergyman's Recreation, Shewing the Pleasure and Profit of the Art of Gardening

John Laurence

The
Clergymans
Recreation.

Pr. for B. Lintot

J. Gribelin sculp.

THE
Clergy-Man's Recreation:

Shewing the

Pleasure *and* Profit

Of the ART of

GARDENING.

Quare agite ò proprios generatim difcite cultus,
Agricolæ, fructufque feros mollite colendo.
Virg. Georg.

By *John Lawrence*, A. M. Rector of *Yel-
vertoft* in *Northampton-fhire*, and fome-
time Fellow of *Clare-Hall* in *Cambridge*.

The Second Edition Corrected.

LONDON:

Printed for BERNARD LINTOTT, between the
Two *Temple-Gates*, in *Fleet ftreet*. MDCCXIV.

Mr. LINTOTT,

SO far as I am Judge, there is more of
the Art of Gardening in this little
Tract, than in all I have yet seen on this
Subject.

March 15. 1713.

L: Loyd.

THE
PREFACE

GARDENING *being of late Years become the general Delight and Entertainment of the Nobility and Gentry, as well as Clergy of this Nation: It is not with great Difficulty that I have comply'd with the Sollicitations and Desires of many of my Friends, to communicate to the Publick some of that Skill which I have acquired therein, by the Observations and Experience of above Twenty Years.*

I am not so vain as to think I am able to teach the great Masters in this Science any new Discoveries concerning the management of the Orangerie, or the Melopieres, or to invent any new and costly Ways for laying out Platforms, and enlarging Gardens: This perhaps has been already done to a Fault; and 'tis this Excess which has ruin'd brave Estates, and consequently has made others afraid of engaging in it. For I could never be of the opinion of a certain Noble Person, who spake very contemptibly of his own Garden, to one that admir'd it. Alas! (says he) This is a small inconsiderable Place, of only Thirty Acres; whereas my Lord —— has above Fourscore

IF once we come to vye with one another, either for exquisite Niceness and Finery, or multitude of Acres;

one

The Preface.

one may easily guess what the consequence of that will be. No; therefore the Design of this is neither to teach the management of Exotick Plants for Green-Houses, nor to recommend any thing over-curious or costly; but only to lay down such Rules as may make Returns both of Profit and Pleasure; And to recommend the Art of managing a Garden to those of my own Order, the Clergy; not to make them envyed by Magnificence, but to make them happy, by loving an innocent Diversion suitable to a grave and contemplative Genius. I would not be understood as if I thought a Divine might not Innocently use many other Diversions; only this I suppose most people will allow, that as there are some Sports and Exercises not suitable to a Divine, so Gardening is a very agreeable and commendable Recreation, viz. Pruning, Planting, Sowing, Grafting and Inoculating, and sometimes digging ad Ruborem, tho' not ad Sudorem. For indeed of all others a Clergy-Man, whose chief and most constant Business is sitting at his Study, most wants Relaxation and some moderate Exercise, to preserve Health. For my own part, I must own that 'tis the best and almost only Physick I take: and if through the rigour or wetness of the Season, I am denyed the benefit of my Garden for some days, and labour under Indispositions; Gods Blessing with a warm and Sun-shiny Day that invites me out, soon sets me to rights again.

THIS perhaps is not every ones Constitution, but thus far almost all are agreed, that the Diversions and Amusements of a Garden, with moderate Exercise, are not only most delightful to those that love them, but most wholesome to those that use them. And because it must be supposed to be Ignorance of the Times and Seasons, and the not knowing

what

The Preface.

what to do in a Garden when there, as to Planting, Pruning, Grafting, &c. which make so many regardless, both of the Pleasure and Profit of this Art; And because I think also that many others have been horribly imposed on, either by the Unskilfulness of the Country Gardiners, or, which is worse, their Knavery; whereby they plant Trees of wrong sorts on wrong Stocks, or not in a right Method and Season, so as to be almost wholly discouraged by not receiving any Fruit of their Labour and Charge; For this reason I venture to communicate some Observations that I have made, which I conceive may be of use to my Brethren, or such other Gentlemen as desire to have a pleasant and profitable Garden, and yet may want Skill enough themselves to manage it with Success.

I confess I cannot but with Grief, look into some Gardens where I find little more than Leaves or half dead Trees, whilst yet the Owner, it may be, loves a Garden as well as my self, and has impatiently expected the Fruits of it for many Years; and yet has only at last bought his Experience with the Loss of all that Time. This I speak as to the choicer sort of Fruit against Walls, where the Disappointment has proceeded from wrong Positions : as for instance, the Buree-Pear against a North or North-East Wall; or from wrong Stocks, as the Apricot on the ordinary Plum Suckers ; Or the being cheated in the sort of Fruit you send for, which is the most common Disappointment of all. And truly this has made me look on with great Compassion, to see Gentlemen thus defeated of their Hopes, almost discouraged against any farther Attempts; because they have already waited so long, even the best (as it is the earliest and most vigorous) part of their Lives without Success. For a wrong sort of Fruit,

or

The Preface

or Fruit upon a wrong Stock will, it may be, draw you
on with Expectation for 4 or 5 or 6 Years to taste its
Fruit, and then possibly you find with Grief, instead of an old
Newington Peach, a dry insipid Nectorine, or instead of
a rich French Pear, a gritty Choak Pear or Warden;
Or else your Tree being on a wrong Stock, will make a shift
to live 4 or 5 Years, and then dye at last. So that in
both these Cases, your best and only Remedy is to take
them up and plant Others; and it may be not without
the same Fear of being deceived again. And yet if they
prove what you expect, here must be 3 or 4 Years more
before you receive Fruit; And I need not tell any one
what a Disappointment it is to lose 8 or 10 Years of the
best part of our Lives in tired and fruitless Expectations. If therefore I shall be able in any measure to re-
move these Fears from those who would otherwise love
these innocent Diversions, and give them better hopes, I
desire what follows may not be thought impertinent or unr
seasonable, though coming from a Clergy-Man.

I have often smiled at the Rebukes I have met with
from some Gardiners, who hate to be inform'd by a Schol-
lar, or to be turned out of their beaten Road by any Body.
What, say they, does this Man come and pretend to teach
us, to make our Masters think we do not understand our
Business? How should he know what Stocks are best for
Trees, or how to prune them? It is fitter for him to be at
his Studies a making Sermons. So that I assure you, if the
Gentleman has not a great deal of Courage, he must be content
to go on in the old way, or very much disoblige his Gardiner.

I am not in the least ashamed to say and own, that
most of the time I can spare from the necessary Care and
Business of a large Parish, and from my other Studies,

is

The Preface.

is spent in my Garden, and making Observations towards the further Improvement thereof. For I thank God this sort of Diversion has tended very much to the ease and quiet of my own Mind, and the Retirement I find therein, by Walking and Meditation, has help'd to set forward many useful Thoughts upon more divine Subjects, as I may perhaps hereafter have occasion to inform the World. In the mean time I cannot but incourage and invite my Reverend Brethren to the Love of a Garden; having my self all along reap'd so much fruit from it, both in a figurative and litteral Sense.

BY the good Providence of God, and the extraordinary uncommon Bounty of a generous Patron, which I always remember with Gratitude, I have been placed where I am now, near Fourteen Years: And it may not be amiss to relate what Difficulties I have all along laboured under, that others may see what is to be done with Care, even on the worst of Soils.

ADJOINING to my House, I found what they used to call a Garden, of about 32 Yards square, mounded round with low Mud-Walls, quite over-run with Couch or Twitch-Grass, Nettles and Gooseberry-Bushes; and, which was a great deal worse, upon a wet white Clay, lying within half a Foot of the Surface. The earnest Desire I always had to have a Garden, made me look on with Grief; but yet I instantly resolved to be doing something, that no time might be lost, towards getting Wall-Fruit if possible.

I was disswaded by most of my Neighbours, as thinking it a very vain attempt, and that I should lose all my Labour and Charge, as others have done. Not yet discouraged, I resolved to pull down the Mud-Wall that faced the

The Preface.

South-East, and to build a Brick one in the stead about Nine Foot high, which I did by the kind Help of my Neighbours, the same Summer I came, and sent for my Trees from London in October, and Planted the Walls with Apricots, best Pears, Vines, Figs, Plums, Cherrys, a Peach and Nectorine. My next Care was to provide a Nursery of all sorts of Stocks for future Planting, as I made Room for them.

WHAT Methods I used to give my self any hopes of Fruit in a Garden, which with respect to the Soil, was made almost invitâ Minervâ, will appear by the following Directions: But I only say here, to encourage my Friends, that in 3 Years time, if not sooner, I began to taste some of the Fruits of my Labours; The fourth Year I was rewarded with Fruit from almost all of them; And ever since I have had Plenty, even greater than I could reasonably expect from all the several sorts, except the old Newington, which I most of all suspected by reason of the Soyl; though even that flourished and bore, but the Fruit was watry and insipid. I have succeeded better in other sorts since.

AS to the Nursery that I formed chiefly from all sorts of Seeds and Stones, I have succeeded so well, that by Grafting and Inoculating thereon, I have for several Years had enough, not only for my own Use in all parts of my Orchard and Kitchen-Garden, but also to oblige my Friends, which is no small part of my Pleasure.

I give these short Hints to shew how adviseable it is, when Persons first come to a Living or an Estate, to begin their Plantations without Doors first, and not, as is usual, fall to Repairs and Alterations within, to the neglect of the Other. What we build or repair, generally

speaking,

The Preface.

speaking, may be finished in a Summer, and we enjoy the Conveniences thereof as soon as finished, and the Workmen have left you: But you must wait some years to see the Fruits of your Plantation, and therefore the sooner it is begun, the more reasonably you may hope to live to enjoy the Benefit and Pleasure of it.

BUT because I represented it as a very difficult and hazardous matter to procure right sorts of Fruit, and upon good Stocks; it may be expected that I should give some Direction and Advice what to do, since it is of so great consequence to be assured of a Skilful as well as a Faithful Nursery-Man. To this I only say, that in such a case as this, the best way is to trust to Men of known Honesty, Skill and Integrity, such as the late Mr. London, and Mr. Wise, have hitherto approved themselves to be; and their Names and Reputation are so well established amongst the Nobility and Gentry, that I hardly think the surviving Person, Mr. Wise, would willingly put a Cheat upon any One that would trust to him. However I should not do Justice to that honest Person I have so long dealt with, and so often recommended, if I should not take occasion here to say, that of above Five Hundred Fruit Trees bought of him, by my self and Friends, I do not remember I ever heard that one of them miscarried through his Fault, or proved otherwise than the kind and sort that was sent for: his Name is Nicholas Parker, Nursery-Man at Strand-in-the-Green in Chiswick-Parish, near London; where I am well persuaded any Gentleman or other may be punctually and faithfully dealt with, though not known to him.

IF any one shall now say upon sight of this little Treatise; That, as a Clergy-Man, I might have imploy'd my

time

The Preface.

time much better than to write about Gardening, I answer;
That it easily appears a great deal of time has not been
spent in composing it; Indeed only a few leisure Hours
in the Winter, for want of Company by way of diversion; not at all interfering with, much less interrup-
ting my proper Studies, or the necessary attendance on
the Duties of my Parish, which I think ought always to
be uppermost, and to lye next the Heart of us the
Ambassadors of Christ, who have so great a Trust and
solemn a Charge committed to us; as, The teaching
others the way of Salvation.

I hope therefore I need not say any thing further by
way of Apology, except it be with respect to the Defects
and Omissions of this small Tract; and These I hope
will be pardoned by the great Masters in this Science, as
coming from a Clergy-Man, who owns he has had greater things to mind. But if I have said any thing here to
perswade those of my own Order to love an agreeable Exercise and Recreation; and have taught them how to make
something of Interest and Pleasure, of those little Paren-
theses of their Lives, which most commonly go for nothing, I shall have gain'd my End, and the Satisfa-
ction I aim at.

THE

THE
Clergy-Man's Recreation:
Shewing the
Pleasure and Profit
Of the Art of
GARDENING.

CHAP. I.

Concerning Preparing the Ground for Planting and Sowing.

THE Method that I shall observe in treating this Subject shall be the same that I would advise all Persons to proceed in, who intend to form a Garden of their own, where it may be, there are little or no Preparations towards it. And I do not intend to direct you to any such Costly Experiments and Rules, as *Mounsieur Quintenye* proposes to his Royal Master; But shall all along have regard not only to the cheapest but also the most Expeditious Methods to procure you the Fruits of your Cost and Labour.

There-

Therefore for the sake of those who must either form a Garden out of their Home-sted, or (which is most common) do find a mounded Place, for a Garden full of little else but noxious and spreading Weeds, I shall lay down the following Rules distinctly to each Case. To the first, who are to form a Garden anew, and intend to build Walls, I say that Thirty or Forty Yards square is abundantly enough for that you intend for your best Garden, where you would have your choicest Fruits and Flowers grow; for more would make you uneasie to have it kept and managed as it ought: If there be no great Inconvenience in it, it will be better to have your Walls face not the four Cardinal Points, but rather between them, *viz.* South-East, South-West, North-East, and North-West; for then the two former will be good enough for the best Fruit; and the two latter good enough for Plumbs, Cherries, and Baking Pears. Only observe this, that instead of building your Wall that faces the North-East, it may be adviseable (to save Charges) to plant a Crab-Hedg of Three Rows, which will be a good Mound, and will quickly grow up to be a better Fence than a Wall against the West, and South-West Winds, which make the greatest destruction in a Garden, and according to the Observations I have made, do blow two parts in three of the whole Year. It may be adviseable also to plant here and there an Elm to be growing up to a greater height. For whatever you do, you must be sure to guard against the Westerly Winds, which blast your Fruit more than those from the East, as they are

much

much more frequent. After your Platform is thus
laid out, and you have difposed your Walks of
Gravel and Grafs as your own Fancy leads you, (for
there is no Mode or Fashion in those things) you
muft then haften to build your Walls, that your
Fruit-Trees may be ready to plant in *October*, and
in the mean time be digging your Ground to mel-
low all Summer and Winter.

There is fome different Method to be ufed by
thofe that find a Garden-place already mounded,
full of noxious Weeds: For their firft care muft be
to deftroy *them*; fo that what is fown or planted
afterwards may not perifh by *their* fpreading luxuriant Growth; feveral Methods have been propofed towards deftroying Weeds, fuch as fowing the
Ground thick with Turnips, Hemp, &c. But I
have found no way fo certain and effectual as laying
the whole Ground fallow all the Summer by digging
it over two or three feveral times, always obferving
to do it in the greateft Heats and Drought. This
not only certainly kills all the Weeds, but it likewife
mellows and enriches the Ground exceedingly, as
all Farmers know very well. Moft are naturally
defirous and greedy to make fome improvement of
their Ground, but if they fow any thing with expectation of Fruit, while 'tis full of Weeds, 'tis but
lofs of time, and they will repent it. I do not fpeak
this with refpect to your Plantation of Fruit-Trees,
either Dwarfs or Wall-Trees. For I would have no
time loft in the Planting of them, that you may the
fooner taft their Fruit: neither will the Method
propofed in the leaft hinder this defign; for you
                                                    may

may with little difficulty clear those particular places of all noxious Weeds (which yet must be done with care) where you intend to Plant your Trees; and yet the rest of the Ground may lye fallow; which leads me to shew you under this Head, what is to be done, before you plant your Trees : For except your Ground be extraordinary good indeed, you must dig a Hole of four Foot square, and two Foot deep, which must be filled up again with Dung and good Mould for each Tree you intend to plant. If your Ground be Marle or stiff Clay (which is my particular misfortune) you must get all the Rubbish you can together, of Lime, Stone, small pieces of Brick and Tyle, Coal-ashes, and Drift Sand to mix with your best Mould and Dung, so that the Clay may not convert it to its own nature; fill up the Hole with this half a Foot higher than the rest of Level, remembring to preserve some of the finest Mould near the Top (free from Dung) to plant your Tree in: But if your Soil be a not over rich or hungry Gravel or Sand, you must fill up the Holes with the best rotten Horse and Cow-Muck you can get, together with the richest Mould. Thus when your Holes are cleaned from Weeds, and prepared and filled up according to the afore-going direction, put an upright Stick in the middle of the Hole for a Mark where to plant the Tree in the order you intend.

But because it is a thing of such great consequence to have your Trees well planted in order to secure their future Growth and Prosperity, I cannot but add one further direction about this matter, which

which long Experience has confirmed to me to be a
good one, *viz.* this; That nothing is more agreeable or fuitable to the Roots of a young Tree than
untry'd Mould or Earth. Such I mean as has not within the compafs of an Age been turned up either
with Plow or Spade, which I fuppofe may eafily be
found in moft Lordfhips: But I would recommend
that particularly which is wont to be call'd a Waft
or Common, whereon Cattel have ufed to ftand either for Shelter or Convenience. The Nature and
Richnefs of this having never been exhaufted by the
luxuriant growth of Plants or Shrubs, or larger
Weeds, there is a ftrange and uncommon Fertility in
it; more I think than is ordinarily to be met with in
any other rich Compofitions of made Earths; At
leaft 'tis fuch as I have found more fuitable for the
growth of young Trees; and therefore the more of
this you put into the Places where you plant, the
better: Always obferving to take off a thin upper
Turf, and then dig only one Spade deep for this
purpofe; and if your Garden-foil be Marl or Clay,
remember (as I obferved before) to mix Coal-afhes of
Drift-Sand with it,otherwife all will quickly be con-
verted to the native circumambient Soil, and thereby your Tree in ten or twelve years time will lan-
guifh, canker, and, it may be, die.

I need not tell you here, that 'tis perfect murde-
ring a young Tree to fet it in the fame Place and
Soil where an old one had grown; and therefore
more than ordinary care is to be taken to replenifh the
Place with this new untried Mould, as far as the old
Roots went, or at leaft as far as new ones need to go.

B

It may not be amiss also to add under this Head, that if your good Soil be very shallow, or that your Garden lye over-wet and moist, it is a very good and safe way to lay Tiles or Bricks all over the bottom of your Trench, to hinder the Roots from striking downwards, and so occasion their spreading into the good Soil. For 'tis a Rule in Gardening, that the more horizontally either Roots or Branches of Fruit-Trees run, the better they answer the purposes of bearing Fruit; as I shall have occasion to observe further under the Head of pruning. I shall conclude this Head with advising those who are so unhappy as to lye upon a spewy, wet, or clay Soil, to make a pretty many convenient Drains, which may be done at a very easie charge, by only digging Trenches two or three Foot deep, leading to the lower Ground, and then pouring in Pebbles or any rough or rubbish Stones: upon which lay some small green Boughs, and throw the Earth again upon them. This I have experienced to last many Years, and will effectually drain your Garden.

C H A P. II.

Of the Method of Planting Fruit-Trees in your Garden.

WHEN you have disposed your Borders according to the aforegoing Directions, great care must be had in the right ordering and dispo-

disposing also your young Trees; for if they be not planted according to Art, *viz.* not rightly ordered in their Roots, nor set at their right Height or due Distances, your Expectations may be in great measure defeated. If therefore your Trees come from the Nurseries about *London*, (as what seems to me most adviseable) the first thing you have to do is to prune their Roots, by taking off all the small Fibres intirely, and shortning the bigger Roots to about six Inches from the Stem; and if they have received any Gall or Wound in their Carriage, that part of the Root must also be cut off: two or three Spurs are sufficient, but if there be more good ones, they may remain pruned as aforesaid. The next thing to be done, by reason of their having been out of the Ground several days, and so are become very dry, is to steep them in some Vessel of Milk and Water, or Dish Water for 24 Hours, which will supple the Roots, and make them apter to strike new Fibres into the Earth when Planted. The Head also must be pruned; but that may be done any time before it begins to shoot in the Spring. A single Branch is sufficient for a Head, and it is not well to leave above two, pruned to about six Inches above the place of Grafting or Inoculation. If it be a Dwarf, place it as upright as you can; If for the Wall, set the Foot as far from the Foundation as conveniently may be, leaning with its top to the Wall.

The afore-going direction about pruning the Roots and Head ought to be particularly regarded, because it is the common Fault of young and unskilful Planters' to be covetous of leaving as much

Head

Head as may be; thinking *That* to be the earliest and most ready way to cover their Walls and to have Fruit; whereas if it does not endanger the Life of the Tree, it is a certain means to retard its Growth, and keep the Walls bare and uncover'd towards the Bottom. Indeed Reason, as well as Experience, tells us that there should be a due proportion between the Roots and the Head; for Nature having received a great check at the Removal of a Tree, its Roots being wounded, shortn'd, and expos'd to the Air, if the Tree should not be eased of that tall Head it got in its prosperity ; (now larger than the injured Roots can supply with Sap) the necessary Consequence would be, that if it should just live, yet it must continue in a weak, languishing and unthriving Condition. However it may easily be perceived by what has been said, that there is a Discretional Power to be used by a Planter with respect to those Trees which are only removed from one part of the Garden to another, taken up with great care, and most of the Mould about the Roots. Such I have my self frequently removed without either pruning Root or Branch, and have succeeded very well; But then this is hardly to be practised on any but small young Trees: And I sometimes do this designedly, with only this View, to check the luxuriant Growth of a too vigorous Tree running altogether into Wood, taking it up carefully, and immediately setting it down again in the very same place, for a reason you'll hear more of, when we come to Pruning.

The

The different nature of Soils is to be regarded as to the height you are to plant a Tree above the Level of your Walks. In a warm dry Soil, a little Elevation does; but in a wet Clay, you cannot ordinarily plant too high, so that you do but in any fort cover the Roots with the best fine Mould, and preferve it moist for one Year, against the fcorching Heats of the Sun, by which means it will be preferved from Canker, and thrive much the fafter, even tho' there fhould appear fome part of the bigger Roots above the Surface; and still remember to allow for the fubfiding of the new Earth, which will deceive you three or four Inches. Be careful to follow thefe Directions, obferving to leave no Vacuities at the Roots, but prefs the fine Mould gently and clofely with your Hand, and you need not fear hardly any fort of our Fruit Trees growing and flourifhing.

But it may not be amifs to fay fomething concerning a fafe Method to keep new planted Trees moist and cool for the firft Year, and if need be, for the fecond. Mr. *Landon* and *Wife* recommend Fern and Straw laid five or fix Inches thick, and two or three Foot every way from the Stem of the Tree, having first laid half-rotten Dung all round the Tree. I very much approve of this, to keep them warm in Winter from the violent Frofts: But the Straw and Dung lying too long together engenders Worms, Ants and other fort of Vermin, very injurious to Roots of Trees: Therefore the beft Method I have found to keep the Roots cool and moist in Summer is to lay Sand in a convenient Circle round the

B 3

Stem

Stem of the Tree, and then pitch or pave it with small Pebbles. Flints or any little smooth Stones, which will not only look beautiful to the Eye, but also effectually answer the end of keeping the Tree cool; and besides, when you water it in the Summer, will help to let in the Water, and keep the Earth from being wash'd away from the Roots.

It is also to be observed that this Method of managing Trees in the planting them will be of the same use with respect to all Ever-greens, which are generally not over forward to thrive after a Removal. I say you must *plant* them after the foregoing Rules, but not *prune* them, especially Hollys and Yews, which have matted Roots, and will hold the Earth to them, sufficient to convey them to small Distances; and if a greater distance is required, they ought to be sent in Pots or Baskets, that neither Root nor Head may be touch'd with a Knife.

As to the Distance in which Fruit-Trees are to be planted against a Wall, *That* is in a great measure to be regulated by the height of the Wall. Four Yards distance will do, if the Wall be ten or twelve Foot high; but if it be but seven or eight Foot high, five Yards distance is the least that can be allowed. Only you are to observe that a Pear, a Plum, an Apricot and a Cherry, require something a greater distance than a Peach or Nectorine; and therefore the lower Walls too are most suitable to the latter, if they have but a good aspect. I cannot but recommend that frugal Method practised by most Gardners near *London*, of planting tall Fruit-Trees, Cherries or Plums, in the intermediate spaces

of

of the Wall, so that both top and bottom will be well nigh furnished in two or three years time. And then as the Dwarfs spread and increase, they take away the tall Ones quite, making Standards of them in Orchards. Except you had rather chuse to plant Vines in those intermediate spaces, which will quickly run up to the top, and bear the second or third Year.

As to the best season for planting, the general Rule to be given for *that*, is from the middle of *October* to the middle of *March*; Only you must be sure to avoid doing any thing of this nature in hard Frosts, and if your Trees in coming down happen to be overtaken by them, your only way is to carry them into Cellars, laying what Mould you can get over their Roots, and plenty of Straw over that, staying till the Frost be gone, that you may plant them safely. Tho' I have said that any time betwixt *October* and *March* be the season of Planting, yet I prefer planting in Autumn rather than Spring for these two following Reasons.

(1.) Because a Tree planted in *October* or *November*, if the Ground be not over moist and cold, will make some little Progress towards its future Growth during the Winter Half-year, its Roots swelling and disposing themselves to put forth those several small Fibres, which are to nourish and support the Tree, and so prepare it for the kinder influences of the Sun in the Spring; when also the Earth will be better fixed and settled about the Roots, so as to keep out the parching Winds of *March* and *April*, often fatal to young Trees as well as new-removed Plants and Flowers.

B 4 (1.) Be-

(2.) Because the Spring is a time when the chief of a Gardeners Work comes on, Digging, Sowing all manner of Seeds, Grafting, and some Pruning and Nailing, therefore it is not desirable to have also the business of Planting Trees to do then, when most of his other Business falls together upon his Hands. We commonly say, what is done in a Hurry is seldom done well, and when Business is once put into good Order; 'tis nigh half done; It makes a great part of a Wise Man's Pleasure and Diversion to have always something to do, but never too much. And methinks we should always choose to have Amusements offer themselves to us, not in a Crowd, but in a regular and orderly Succession. Besides, some Intervals of Time betwixt one sort of Business in a Garden and another are very desirable to a good Man, who knows how to recapitulate all his Pleasures in a devout lifting up of his Hands, his Eyes, and his Heart to the great and bountiful Author of Nature, who gives Beauty, Relish and Success to all our honest Labours. These grateful Thoughts, I own, these Contemplations in my own Garden, (with the Hopes of living in Paradise it self, where both natural and revealed Religion will be better understood than they are at present) give me a comfortable Taste of the Divine Goodness and Bounty, which alone give the truest Relish to every Thing else.

But to return, and to conclude this Chapter, your Trees being planted according to the foregoing Directions, and standing with their tall Heads till the

the beginning of *March*, tack'd to the Wall to prevent their being shaken with Winds, you are then to shorten their Heads according to the Rule already laid down; but great care must be had that it be done with a sharp Knife and a steady Hand, for fear of disturbing the Root: Cut it slopewise, the slope facing the Wall.

CHAP. III.

Concerning the most agreeable Disposition of a
GARDEN.

AFTER an early and diligent care to furnish our Walls with Trees planted after the best Method, and in the properest Season, we will commit them to the prolifick Blessing of Heaven, that gives Life and fruitful Seasons, and proceed to consider what is to be done next to make the other parts of the Garden agreeable as well as profitable. My purpose is not to give you all the varieties of Platforms, nor to lay out great Designs. Every one may easily please himself in a Form that strikes most his own Fancy in so small a piece of Ground as I suppose a Garden need contain: Only, it may be, I may happen to give some useful Hints to those who are desirous to hear what others can say to direct their own Fancies:

I would say then, that if I were to chuse a Figure that could be as cheap and as easily had as another,

it

it should be a Square, or rather an Oblong-Square, leading from the middle of my House; a Gravel-Walk in the middle, with narrow Borders of Grass on each side for Winter-use, and on each side of them Rows of all the Varieties of Winter-greens set at due Distances, which will appear with an agreeable Beauty from the House all the Year. But then I say too, that I should be under no sort of Uneasiness to be confin'd to an irregular piece of Ground, which may be made to have its Beauties as well as the most regular. Strait Lines bring any thing into Order, and I see not but a Triangle in a Garden has its Beauty as well as a Square, and yet an irregular piece of Ground may be made to have Both by vertue of strait Lines, *viz.* Borders and Walks.

I confess indeed an Irregularity is not so easily hid in a little Ground as it is in a Garden of larger extent, where long Walks, and tall Hedges interrupt a distant and thorough View, and where, though the Walks and Hedges terminate in obtuse or acute Angles, no ways disagreeable to the Eye; yet you are insensibly led into new and unexpected Beauties still as you advance. Three or four Walks and double Rows of Hedges may be there contrived to open themselves at once to view, all terminating in the place where you stand, and the Triangular Spaces by an ingenious Fancy may be there agreeably disposed and filled up either with Borders of Flowers, or with Dwarff-Trees, or with Flowring Shrubs, or with Ever-Greens; or lastly with a little Wilderness of Trees rising one above another, till you come to the point of a tall one in the middle;

this

this laſt may be made to look very beautiful with
Charge and Care to clip them; for I am now got into a large Garden that requires a good Purſe; and
therefore before I part with it, I will only add, that
methinks Gentlemen ſhould not be over ſollicitous
at great Charges, ſo to level or ſquare their Gardens
as to throw them open to one ſingle view from the
Houſe; (which doubtleſs may be made a very beautiful one) becauſe it may be worth while to conſi-
der, whether matters may not be ſo contrived, as to
afford you many uncommon Prettineſſes wholly ow-
ing to the Irregularity or Unevenneſs of the Ground.
Inſomuch that every little advance you make, you ſhall
be preſented with ſomething new to ſtrike the Fancy.
    But altho' (as you ſee) Irregularities are beſt diſ-
guiſed and ſet off in a large Plot of Ground, yet
even in a leſſer Garden, an irregular Form, if it be
not very aukward indeed, may be reduced to a Re-
gularity ſufficiently agreeable as well as uſeful, as
may be ſeen by the following plain Scheme.

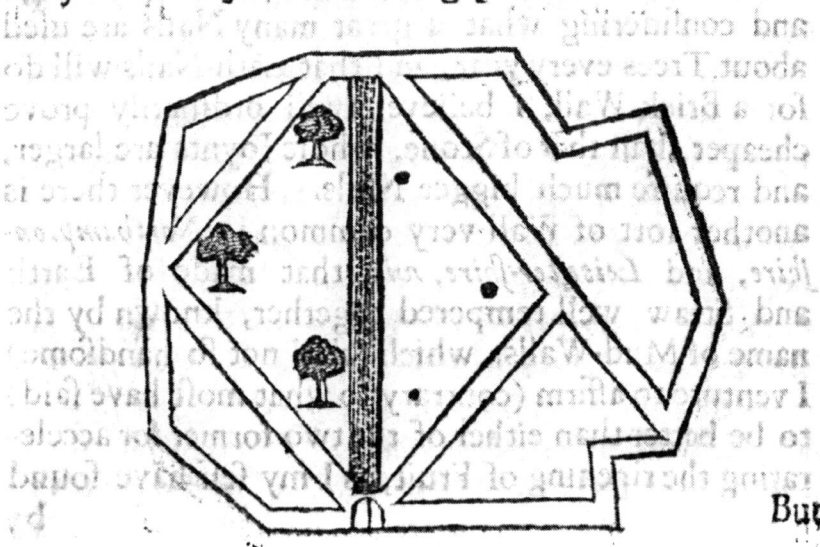

But

But it is seldom one shall meet with so irregular a piece of Ground ready walled out and designed for a Garden, and it can hardly be supposed any Lover of Order would chuse to make it so, if he could easily help it.

As to the Walks, every one knows that both Grass and Gravel are very agreeable, when they are well kept; and therefore it is convenient to have a mixture of both; and I think seven foot wide is sufficient for either, in such a Garden as I am supposing. Only it may not be amiss to add, that it will be some advantage to your Fruit, if you contrive those Walks that run parallel to your South-East, or South-West Walls to be Gravel, because the Sun will certainly thereby reflect an additional Heat to them. I have said nothing about the properest Materials for Walls, because I suppose every one will chuse to make use of such as are nearest at Hand, and what the Country affords. Brick is undoubtedly the handsomest and most commodious for Nailing; and considering what a great many Nails are used about Trees every year, and that Lath-Nails will do for a Brick-Wall, I believe 'twill ordinarily prove cheaper than that of Stone, whose Joynts are larger, and require much bigger Nails. However there is another sort of Wall very common in *Northampton-shire*, and *Leicester-shire*, *viz.* that made of Earth and Straw well tempered together, known by the name of Mud-Walls, which (tho' not so handsome) I venture to affirm (contrary to what most have said) to be better than either of the two former for accelerating the ripening of Fruit, as I my self have found

by

by experience. The Fruit indeed is fometimes apt to be foiled by great dafhes of Rain: But there is not much in that, and the Objection is wholly taken away in fuch Fruit as requires paring, as Peaches, and Pears, &c. If the Walls be made of very good Earth and well temper'd, Nails will do, otherwife I ufe Pegs of Wood, fuch as are ufed for bad Walls for faftening the Branches. The large Coping of Straw that is laid upon thefe fort of Walls is no fmall Advantage to the Fruit in fheltering them, and keeping off all perpendicular Rains. But as I obferved, they are not veryfightly; and thofe who will regard Beauty fhould have Brick Walls.

It is not convenient to have the Borders under the Wall too wide; three Foot is fufficient, that you may not at every turn be forced to ftand upon them to nail or gather. There are great Varieties of A-romaticks, and other Plants recommended to fupport Borders, fuch as *Thyme, Winter favory,* feveral forts of *Sedums*; but none I approve of fo much as Dwarf-Box, in that it is fo durable, and fo eafily kept with one clipping in a Year.

Great care muft be taken that no fort of tall Trees be fuffered to grow in any of the oppofite Borders or intermediate fpaces, fo that the fhade of them reach to any of the South-Eaft, or South-Weft Walls, whereby your Expectations of having good or early Fruit might eafily be fruftrated; thofe pla-ces fo near your Walls would be better filled with round Dwarfs kept hollow in the middle; or rather with flat ones humouring the Borders with their Horizontal Branches; and what forts are propereft for thefe I fhall tell you in a Chapter by it felf.   I

I never thought it any difparagement to my beſt Garden, where I make my Soil commonly better than ordinary, to ſow in ſome of the intermediate Spaces, ſome of thoſe Reptiles uſeful in the Kitchen, *viz.* Carrots, Onions, Parſnips, Spinage, *&c.* that it may anſwer its purpoſe, a profitable as well as pleaſant Garden ; for theſe not growing tall, but kept clean from Weeds, are no unſeemly ſight at all, but rather make a pleaſing variety amongſt Trees and Flowers. Indeed I commonly chuſe to baniſh out of this Garden all thoſe prouder taller Things, Peas, Beans, Kidney-beans, and Cabbages, which are not ſo ſightly, and look more ruinous ; and therefore aſſign them a place by themſelves at a diſtance.

It is needleſs to add any more Particulars under this Head ; every ones own Fancy muſt ſupply what ſeems a Defect, for 'twould be endleſs to ſpeak to all thoſe Caſes that an uneven irregular piece of Ground might ſeem to require.

CHAP. IV.

Of NURSERIES.

AFTER we have given our ſelves ſome reſpite from the great buſineſs and concern of Planting and diſpoſing the Ground according to our own Fancy (for that's the Beauty that pleaſes moſt)

most) we must by no means forget, as soon as possible, to begin to raise Nurseries of all sorts of Trees, which will be growing up to exercise our Art and Skill, and supply all our future Wants, which also will still answer our purpose of Pleasure and Profit. And I am not for throwing such Nurseries too far from our daily and constant Inspection, but am willing, if possible, to let the chief of them have a place in the best Garden, least they be forgotten and neglected; for which purpose an irregular Figure in a Garden is peculiarly subservient, affording several little triangular Spaces proper to raise the several Nurseries we shall have occasion for.

Now there are at least two distinct places to be allotted for the purpose of Nurseries, *viz.* one for tall Standards, Apples, Pears, Oaks, Elms, Ashes, Sycamores and Limes, *&c.* which may be most proper to be at some distance from the House; and another for Dwarfs, such as you intend for Peaches, Apricots, Pears, Plums and Cherries. And I would also have a third added for all sorts of Ever-greens by themselves. Now these two latter may be very properly made in some such By-places, as most Gardens will afford, and that with no Interruption to the Beauty of it.

The Nursery you intend for the taller Standards should be made in a good rich light Soil from the several sorts of Seeds peculiar to their kind, sown in *October* or *November*. Crabs and wild Pear-Kernels are to be prefer'd for Stocks to make Apples and Pears. Limes and Elms are to be raised from planted Suckers; and if you sow Walnuts, 'tis adviseable

to

to sow them with the Green Shell upon them to preserve them from Mice in the Winter. If this Nursery be well managed and kept clean from Weeds for two years, the third year the Crabs and Pears will be fit for Grafting and Inoculating, the Method of which I shall briefly shew you in a Chapter by it self.

It will be convenient to have the Nursery for Dwarfs by it self, that they may not be overtopt by taller Trees. And you are to observe that the Stones of Peaches and Apricots are by no means proper to raise those sorts of Trees good or lasting: But for this purpose you must get together a good Quantity of Stones taken either from the Pear-plum, Muscle or *Bonum magnum* Plum, which have been found by long Experience to be better and more lasting than any other. The not being careful about this matter has been the Occasion of great disappointments; the Trees often dying after two or three years, tho' the Stocks have been alive. Black Cherries also are the only Stocks, whereon to raise all the several sorts of Cherries, But the best Plum will do on any ordinary Plum or Sucker. Tho' it is not so adviseable to use Suckers even from the best sorts, because they will be constantly apt to put forth such plenty of Suckers themselves, and so the Vigour of the Tree may be too much exhausted that way.

The third Nursery also that I mentioned of all sorts of Ever-Greens is a very pleasant and profitable One, and deserves a place in our Garden; but it requires something a different Management from the two former. For which purpose you must provide

your

your felf with a fufficient Quantity of the Seeds or Berries of Holly, Yew, and Juniper, which you may put into diftinct but ordinary Pots or Boxes, putting alfo fome fine Mould over them in the Pot, and fo bury them for one Year. For if you fhould fow them (as other Seeds) immediately, they would not come up the firft Year, by which means you would lofe the Ground that Year, and have befides the trouble and charge of keeping it clear from Weeds. Whereas by thus laying them in heaps for one Year in any By-place, you will have them all ready by the following Spring to fow out in order, and they will come up as other Seeds; only you muft be very careful to keep thefe Beds clean from Weeds, which do fo eafily choke all Plants of fo flow a Growth. A flow Growth indeed they have for the firft two Years, but after that, they will recompence all your Labour and Care by their Beauty, Ufefulnefs and vigorous Growth: whereas fhould you content your felf to get thefe forts of Plants out of the Woods or Hedges, they will mightily deceive you. The greateft part of them will die, and the reft will only toll you on with Expectations of their Growth, and yet will rarely prove vigorous and thriving Plants.

This laft Nurfery will be of great Ufe to give new Beauties to your Garden as Occafion ferves, or as your Fancy fhall lead you to adorn it with feveral forts of Ever-green Hedges Among which, none in my mind is to be compared to the Yew, which is (as I may fay) fo tonfile, and grows fo very thick and beautiful with Clipping, and withal bids defyance

C

to the hardeſt Winters, that it is the beſt and moſt laſting Ornament in a Garden. To make one in love with theſe Hedges, you need only take a Walk either in Paradiſe, or the Phyſick-Gardens at *Oxford*, where you are preſented with all that Art and Nature can do to make theſe things moſt agreeable to the Eye. Indeed the Yew is a Plant that loves Uniformity, and is naturally apt to grow regular, and withal ſo intire that it is no very difficult matter to diſpoſe it either for Hedges or Pyramids.

Your Hollys will be beſt employ'd for Stocks to raiſe the ſeveral variegated ſorts by Grafting and Inoculation, which, tho' now common, are no inconſiderable Ornament, to a Garden, making their beſt Shew, when all other things have loſt their Glory; eſpecially when they happen to be full of Red Berries, which make a moſt pleaſing mixture with White or Yellow, and Green Leaves.

I ought to tell you in this place that Firrs and Pines are to be raiſed from thoſe little Seeds taken out of their large Apples, and they will come up the firſt Year, and will quickly make Beautiful Trees, eſpecially in a cold Clay. *Philerea's* and *Pericanthia's* will do beſt from Layers. And as for Vines and Figs, the Culture and Encreaſe of them is ſo eaſily had from Layers and Suckers, that you need not give your ſelf any further trouble about them.

CHAP.

CHAP. V.

Of PRUNING.

IT is of all others the most important Concern of a Lover of a Garden, to know how to prune his Fruit-Trees seasonably, and according to Art; that when he comes to examine them at the time of Fruit, he may find something more than Leaves or Wood. And yet I can by no means think it so difficult a matter to do, as *Monsieur Quintinye* would make one believe by his tedious and enigmatical way of Writing on this Subject, which (as far as I can see) has rather perplex'd than inform'd his Reader. I have had twenty Years experience in this matter, and if I can but speak intelligibly, (as I hope I may) I question not but to make others perform and practice as successfully as I have done my self. So great a desire have I that the Love of Gardening may prevail, that it be not tired with great Charge and little Profit, but be rewarded with good as well as much Fruit. Now in the Business of Pruning it is a hard matter to speak to all cases in exact method, or in the Order of Time, I shall therefore first lay down some general Rules as the fixt Laws whereby every one should govern himself in the management of his Fruit-Trees, either Dwarfs, or those against the Wall, and then proceed to some

C 2   other

other particular Directions that ought to be well regarded for each particular fort, tho' they have not ordinarily been taken notice of. To which purpose it is to be obferv'd.

(1.) That the more the Branches of any Tree are carried Horizontally, the more apt and the better difpofed that Tree is to bear Fruit, and confequently the more upright and perpendicular the Branches are led, the more difpofed that Tree is to encreafe in Wood and lefs in Fruit.

This is what I have long experienced to be true, and (as I conceive) the reafon of it feems to be, That by bending down the Branches of a Tree from a perpendicular to an Horizontal pofture, you thereby check the Sap, or free Circulation of it; (fot that it doth circulate I fhall fhew you in another place) which Circulation when Nature performs moft freely, tends to Growth and Encreafe in Wood; but when it any way fuffers a check either by Art or by Accident in the Body or Root, lefs vigorous and luxuriant Shoots are form'd, and confequently more bearing Buds.

(2.) As a confequence of the aforegoing Propofition, you are ever to take care to keep the middle of a Tree free from great Wood, or thick Branches; but as thefe encreafe and grow upon you, cut them out intirely; there is no Fear but the place will be filled up again quickly with better and more fruitful Wood. In Dwarfs you are to keep all open, intirely free from Wood, leaving only Horizontal Branches. And in your Wall-Trees, if you do but take care to furnifh your Wall with Horizontal

Branches

Branches, Nature will make an abundant provision for the middle; and therefore you muſt chuſe diſcreetly, ſuch as are not over vigorous Shoots, to furniſh you with bearing Branches; a defect of which, or the want of plenty of Bloſſoms in any Fruit-Tree is (generally ſpeaking) a Reproach to the Skill of the Gardener. For tho' he cannot command Fruit from Bloſſoms on the account of bad and unkind Seaſons, and ſo cannot have it *when* he pleaſes, yet he may in a manner have it *where* he pleaſeth, and keep almoſt all parts of the Tree in a bearing ſtate.

(3.) Another general Rule to be obſerved is, to take care your Tree be not over full or crowded with Wood, no not even with bearing Branches, as is too frequently ſeen in the Management of Peaches, Nectorines and Cherries. Nature cannot ſupply a ſufficient Quantity of ſuitable Juices for them, and then the conſequence will be that none of them will be well ſupply'd, but the Bloſſoms will either drop off, or the Fruit will dwindle to nothing. However this is certain that a convenient ſpace between one Branch and another is moſt proper, a Multitude and Confuſion of Branches crowding one upon another, producing neither ſo much nor ſo good Fruit. So croſſing one Branch over another is reckoned very unſeemly, and is indeed contrary to the Rules of Art. But yet this is not to be thought ſo frightful a Sight, that we muſt conſtantly avoid it, even to the ſuffering void Spaces and Barrenneſs in the Wall, which is a greater Evil. A ſlender bearing Branch may often well enough ſteal behind the main Body of

C 3

the

Tree, or fome of its larger Branches, and not offend the Eye at all; but may gratiffe the Tafte at the End of the Year. But ftill this Practice muft not be made too bold with, for fear of Confufion.

Laftly, I fhall only add for a General Rule, that all ftrong and vigorous Branches are to be left longer than weak and feeble Ones on the fame Tree, confequently the Branches of a fickly Tree are to be Pruned fhorter and fewer in number than thofe on a ftrong healthful Tree. Methinks I need not add that all Branches fhooting directly forward from Trees growing againft a Wall are to be cut off clofe to the Branch from whence they come; as alfo all Branches proceeding from the Knob, whereon the Stalk of a Pear grew, are to be intirely taken off; but not the Knob it felf. After having given thefe general Directions, I am perfwaded an ingenious Lover of a Garden, by the help of fome Obfervations that he muft have made of his own, might manage the Bufinefs of Pruning with tolerable good fuccefs: But becaufe there are fome Peculiarities belonging to the management of almoft every kind of Fruit-Tree, (fuch I now mean as grow againft a Wall) I fhall fpeak diftinctly and particularly to each of them what I have found by Experience to be a good and fafe Method of Pruning.

The VINE.

I fhall begin with the Vine, which of all others needs Pruning moft, and tho' it is the eafieft performed, yet (as far as my Obfervation has gone) it is leaft underftood. Our Climate is not fo favourable,

vourable, or the Sun over bountiful of his ripening Heats, but there is need of all the care and the greatest Art to cultivate and help Nature forward in bringing Grapes to any Degree of Perfection in *England.* However this is to be done most Years with some Diligence and Skill. We will then begin with the Vine in the condition it is commonly left in *November,* which, if the Tree has any thing of Youth and Vigour, is confused and ruinous enough, tho' it has been carefully managed the preceding Summer, the Vine putting out the most and the longest Shoots of any other Tree. After therefore you have taken special notice of the first and third general Directions already laid down, you must observe this also peculiar to the Vine: That the lesser and weaker Shoots never bear any Fruit, and therefore must intirely be cut off, inasmuch as they would only tend to weaken the Tree, in drawing away that Sap that should go to nourish the Fruit-branches, which are those of the most vigorous sort; and therefore must carefully be preserved, leaving only 4 or 5 Buds or Eyes of the last Year's Shoot; for if you should leave more, they would only exhaust the Sap in vain, the first and second Eyes only bearing Fruit, and sometimes the third, from the extreme part of the Branch. Indeed when a Vine has put forth a more than ordinary vigorous Shoot, and you can carry it Horizontally into a void place, it will sometimes bear in five or six of the extreme Eyes, and so may be left longer, but this is not ordinarily to be practised. A Vine must lye thinner of Wood than any other Tree, therefore

you

you muſt carefully view what old Wood may be intirely ſpared, and how you can conveniently fill that Space with neighbouring vigorous Shoots, ſtill obſerving every Year to preſerve the new Wood, and to cut out the old. This firſt Pruning of the Vine may be done any time before *February*; but later than that is not adviſeable, leſt it bleed in the Spring, which it will be very apt to do at thoſe places, where you have cut off any thick Branches.

There is alſo a ſecond and third Pruning to be performed on a Vine: The Second is to be done about the middle of *May*, when the Bunches of Grapes are perfectly formed, and the Branch has ſhot two or three foot' long; then pinch off the Branch about ſix Inches above the Fruit, and nail or any way faſten it cloſe to the Wall, ſo that the Fruit may touch if poſſible. The fruitleſs Branches may be let alone to the third Pruning at *Midſummer*, when all muſt be re-examined; for then you are to unburthen the Vine of that multitude of luxuriant Branches it is apt to put forth and to ſhorten them to a convenient length, to let in the Rays of the Sun towards ripening the Fruit; tho' you are to take notice, that it is not convenient to have the Fruit too much expoſed for fear of cold Nights and Rains.

A vigorous Vine will ſtill require a fourth Pruning about *Auguſt*, when it will have ſhot out long Shoots from the Extremity of the laſt Pruning, which therefore muſt be ſhortned again, and ſome of the Leaves diſcreetly pluck'd away from before the Fruit.

There

There is a more than ordinary Neceffity for carefully minding and managing the Vine, becaufe all we can do is little enough to get ripe Fruit efpecially fome Years. and on a bad Soil : But even with both thofe Difadvantages, with a little Diligence and timely Care there has feldom been a Year but I have had good Grapes, and moft Years great plenty. I have try'd fome Experiments for accelerating the ripening of Grapes, as putting the Fruit in *June* into an empty Flask; and running the Branches upon the Tiles of the Houfe, or on a Slope-Wall, but neither anfwered my Expectation. The Grapes indeed ripened in the Flask rather fooner, but then they were apt to be mouldy, for want of free Air, and had an infipid Tafte ; and the Slopes, tho' they admitted more of the Sun's Rays, yet they fubjected the Fruit more to the Rains, Dews, and cold Nights, which (as far as I could fee) overpower'd the greater Blefling of the Sun. To fo little purpofe is it for Men of Theory * to philofophize about thefe matters, without having had fome Experience, and Knowledge in the Practice.

The PEACH and NECTORINE.

Both thefe require the fame Culture and Management, and therefore I put them together; and if the general Rules already laid down be but carefully obferved, there will not need much to be faid

---

* As an Ingenious Author has done, who has wrote a Book in *Quarto*, to fhew in a Mathematical way the great Advantage of Slope-walls.

towards the Government and fuccefsful Pruning of thefe, which are fo apt to put forth plenty of bearing Branches after the fecond or third Year of Planting, that you may eafily make choice of thofe that are good and healthful. If thefe Trees make too much haft to bear, *that* is a bad fign of Weaknefs, and they muft be managed accordingly, by plucking off all or moft of the Blofloms or Fruit, and Pruning fhort. This is a very eafie management, all the difficulty is, when a Peach is overvigorous, for then Nature is apt to make great confufion, and it requires fome Skill to know what to chufe, and what to refufe. You muft therefore be fure to cut out what great Wood can conveniently be fpared, and what remains muft be left the longer ten or twelve Inches of the laft Years Shoot, not forgetting that in two or three Years it muft be cut intirely out, when you can otherwife furnifh your Wall with fmaller Wood. Fruit-bearing Branches, which are very eafie to be known by their full and fwelling Buds, are not generally to be fuffered above five or fix Inches. Thefe (as I obferved are always of the weaker fort, and of the preceding Year's Shoot. You muft take care to cut out all dead Wood, and yellow faplefs Shoots; which that you may be fure to do, it is good for this and other reafons to ftay till the hard Frofts are over before you Prune a Peach, which muft be done with a fharp Knife too, otherwife Strings of the Bark will be left behind; a Pen-knife indeed is moft proper for the fmall bearing Branches. All *Autumn* Shoots muft be rejected as ufelefs and unprofitable. When

you

you have thus trim'd and formed your Tree into Beauty and Order, you have little else to do at it (except the thinning your young Fruit where more than two grow of a heap together) till *Midsummer,* when you must shorten the Shoots discreetly, and fasten them to the Wall; no matter in what Order, because that must be altered the next Pruning; Only you must take care to let the Fruit see the Sun, as soon as 'tis partly come to its bigness, which will give it its proper beautiful Colour, and Maturity also.

After what has been here said, I cannot think it necessary to add any thing particularly with respect to the Apricot, that requiring the same management as the Peach, except that there is no danger of its bearing too soon, and that it is something more apt to run into Wood, which therefore must be particularly considered and guarded against.

The PEAR.

There is no Tree requires the exact and careful Observation of those general Rules laid down so much as the Pear, which in free and rich Soils is apt to be unruly and ungovernable, running altogether into Wood, and luxuriant Branches. It is commonly too proud for a Wall, but yet for the sake of that Noble Fruit which some kinds produce by the Help of a Wall, it is worth while to humble him and keep him in Order. For which purpose (besides what has been already said) I sometimes plash the most vigorous Branches, cutting them, near the place from whence they Shoot, more than half through, which effectually checks its Vigour, and consequently
                                                renders

renders it more disposed to make weaker Shoots and form bearing Buds. This method of Plashing is also of singular use, when you would avoid Barrenness, and have only an aukward Branch to make use of to fill the Vacancy; For by this means you may reduce it to what Order you please, so as to answer your purpose and reward you with Fruit. But you are to take notice that this is not to be practised on any Tree but the Pear and Plum; the Trial would be too dangerous on the Peach or Apricot, because they would be apt to put out Gum at those places, and so endanger killing the whole Branch.

I am aware that many recommend Grafting the Pear on a Quince-stock, which indeed effectually cures too great Luxuriancy and Growth, and may for a time answer the purpose of bearing quickly (which therefore may make it worth while for them that have a great deal of room to have some of these) but they are not long-lived, do not bear such fair large Fruit, nor make such handsome regular Trees, as those Grafted on a Pear stock, which I therefore chuse to recommend to all those, who have not room to try doubtful Experiments.

You will easily distinguish the bearing Buds of a Pear-tree, as soon as the Leaves are off in *November*, which are much fuller and more swelled than others; which is to be carefully minded that you do not cut them off in your Pruning. All false Wood, or, as others call them, Water-shoots are to be taken away, being easily distinguished by their having Eyes at much greater distance than ordinary from one another: These are found in most vigorous Trees, especially

pecially Peaches. The Cock-spur is also to be taken off, *viz.* The Extremity of the last Years Pruning. It is to be managed as the Peach in the Summer.

The F I G.

As this Fruit is commonly little known, and less valued by any but those who have *Gustum Eruditum* (in *Petronius*'s Phrase); so (as far as my Observation has gone) the management of the Tree seems to be as little understood. For as I have hitherto given Directions for the right Pruning of other sorts of Trees, so I must here direct and recommend the not Pruning at all. The not understanding of which has to my Knowledge been the occasion of that Barrenness so visible in many Noblemens and Gentlemens Gardens. There is no Tree that doth generally produce more certain and plentiful Crops than this, if it be rightly managed, or rather if you keep the Knife from it.

But when I say it must not be Pruned, I only mean that its tender Branches are not to be shortn'd, as in other Trees; because it is plain it puts forth its Fruit chiefly at the Extremities of the last Year's Shoot, commonly at the three last Eyes; any part of which if you take away, you cut off and destroy so much Fruit. But yet this must not be supposed to hinder you from taking out the great Wood intirely, to avoid Confusion; and also to cut some of the weak smaller Shoots close to the great Wood, these being of no use but to exhaust Sap. Whatever therefore you cut from the Fig, you must do it as

close

close to the Root, or any great Wood as you can, and that no earlier than the latter end of *March*, for fear of Frosts and Cold Rains: Only it is adviseable to tack its best and biggest Branches close to the Wall in *November*, that they may be the better sheltered from the extreme Frosts in the Winter. Be sure to keep it free from Suckers, which this Tree is apt to put forth plentifully. And I think there needs nothing further to be said for the Government of this Tree, if the three first General Rules be but observed as they ought.

Cherries and Plums require little Skill to make them bear against a Wall in almost any Soil, and therefore there needs nothing to be added to the general Observations laid down. I shall only take notice before I conclude this Chapter, that both Winter and Summer, *Bon-Cretien* Pears, want more Room to spread and extend themselves than any other; and therefore if you expect them to bear, you must allow them Elbow-room and Height too; for if you should confine them by short Pruning, they will grow Knotty, and full of Wood without Fruit. I have my self seen the Summer *Bon Cretien*, in the Garden of my worthy Friend, Dr. *Wickart*, now Dean of *Winchester*, bear plenty of noble large Fruit, betwixt twenty and thirty Foot high. There also I have eaten excellent Figs, from a prosperous Tree, even the same that afforded some to King *James* I. near a Hundred Years ago, as appears (I think) from a *Memorandum* on the Wall.

CHAP.

CHAP. VI.

Of Grafting and Inoculating.

THESE two Operations in Gardening are pretty Philosophical Entertainments to a Lover of Curiosities in Art and Nature, and therefore tho' they have been fully treated of by others, yet because they make up so great a part of a Gardener's Diversion and Pleasure at two several Seasons of the Year, I shall describe and explain the Method of performing both distinctly, that this small Treatise may not be thought defective in so considerable a Point.

There are several Ways of Grafting, but I shall mention only two, that I think most proper to the several kinds of Trees. The first is that common way of Slit-grafting, which is performed on Pear, Cherry, and Plum-stocks, especially if they are of any bigness; by first chusing a smooth place in the Stock where you would graft, cutting the Head off slopewise; then *even* the Top of the Slope Horizontally with your Knife, making a Slit down the middle of the Stock discreetly with a strong Knife, or otherwise; then prepare your Scion taken from a vigorous Shoot of the aforegoing Year, slopeing it on each side from a Bud or Eye, so that it may conform it self to the Slit in the Stock, the Bark of

Scion

Scion and Stock closing exactly. Let it be daub'd pretty thick over with Clay tempered with short Hay, taking care not to disturb the Scion, which must not be left with above three or four Eyes above the Stock. The other way is much preferable to this, but can ordinarily be perform'd only on Apples and Hollys, the Bark in others not handsomely parting from the Wood, as it must. The way is to cut off the Head of the Stock slopewise, *&c.* as before, and instead of flitting the Stock, flit only the Bark a little above an Inch on the back-side of the Slope; then prepare your Scion made with a flat Slope about an Inch long ending on a point, and begun from the back side of an Eye; but because it may disturb the thin End of the Scion to raise the Bark of the Stock, where you made the Slit, get any other piece of smooth Wood cut slopewise as the Scion, and thrust it down betwixt the Wood and the Bark, which you will find readily to part, and then put in your Scion ready prepared, the Top of the Slope being thrust as low as the top-surface of the Stock. Clay it over as before, and leave as many Eyes. This I find to be almost a never failing way for Apples and Hollys, and I prefer it to the other, because it doth not give so grievous a Wound to the Stock by flitting it, which sometimes proves fatal. Besides, in this last way the Scion does much sooner heal over and cover the Stock, whereby the Union is intirely compleated.

The first Operation must be performed on Pears, Cherries, and Plums the latter end of *February* or

begin-

beginning of *March* ; but Hollys and Apples muſt
not be Grafted till the beginning of *April* ; it is convenient that your Scions be cut off a Fortnight or
three Weeks before you uſe them, laid in the ſhade.

But notwithſtanding both theſe Ways may prove
ſafe and proper Methods for propagating thoſe ſeveral kinds of Fruits, yet I much rather prefer, and
therefore recommend that other Operation call'd
Inoculation or Budding, the Method of which I
ſhall now deſcribe : Cut off a vigorous Shoot, from
a Tree you would propagate, any time a Month before, or a Month after *Midſummer* ; then chuſe out
a ſmooth place in your Stock, (which ſhould not
be of above three or four Years Growth) making a
down right ſlit in the Bark of it a little above an Inch
long, and another Croſs-wiſe at the bottom of that
to give way to the opening the Bark. Then with
your Penknife (not too ſharp at the point) looſen
gently the Bark from the Wood on both ſides, beginning at the bottom ; which done, prepare your
Bud taken from the aforeſaid vigorous Shoot, which
muſt be cut off with a ſharp Penknife, entring pretty deep into the Wood, as much above as below
the Bud, to the length of the ſlit in the Stock as near
as you can gueſs. After the Bud is thus cut off,
with the point of the Penknife and your Thumb,
take out the woody part of the Bud, and if in doing
this the very Eye of the Bud come out and leave a
deep Hole, throw it away and take another. Then
put this Bud in between the Bark and the Wood of
the Stock at the Croſs-ſlit already opened, leading
it upward by the Stalk where the Leaf grew, till it

D   exactly

exactly closes: Then bind it about with coarse Woollen Yarn, the better to make all parts of it close exactly, that the Bud may incorporate it self with the Stock, which it will do in three Weeks time, when you must loosen the Yarn, that it do not gall the place too much as it will be apt to do in a vigorous Stock. This Operation is best perform'd in a cloudy day, or at an Evening; and you are to observe the quicker it is done, the better it will succeed. For tho' a pretty many words are necessary to describe the method of doing it, yet after a little practice, and that you are become ready at the work, thirty Inoculations may be done in an Hour: But you may take notice that it is convenient to put in two or three Buds into one Stock, especially Peaches and Nectorines, that you may have the better Hazard of having one hit, which is enough.

Peaches and Nectorines, and Apricots are not to be raised any other way but by Inoculation, and as for Pears, Cherries, Hollys and Plums, tho' (as I have shewn you) they may be Grafted, yet I prefer Inoculating them for these following Reasons.

(1.) Because it is the surest and less hazardous way; nay, if the Stock be but vigorous and not over-big, it is almost a never failing way; for by putting in two or three Buds into one Stock, it will seldom so happen but one of them will hit, and that's enough; whereas in Grafting you are forced to make a dangerous Experiment by cutting off the Head of the Stock, and if the Scion do not take, the Season is lost, and your Stock maimed.

(2.) I

(2.) I prefer Inoculation, becaufe it may be performed by any Gentleman himfelf with more Pleafure and
lefs danger to his Health. It requires no Dawbing
with Clay; only a Penknife and a little Woollen-
Yarn, which are both portable, and therefore always ready to be made ufe of, whenever his Medita-
tions fhall give way to his Pleafure. Befides, this
Operation is perform'd in Summer and warm Wea-
ther, when it is healthful as well as pleafant to be bu-
fied in a Garden with fome fuch little Amufement.
Whereas the Seafon of Grafting is in the Spring,
when there is more danger of taking Cold in a Nurfery where you muft expect wet Feet and dirty
Hands.

Laftly, if you begin to bud in *June*, and you find
it doth not fucceed, (as you may find in three
Weeks) you may make a fecond Attempt the fame
Year on the fame Stock, and that with very good
Succefs : For in fome cafes a difappointment is very
undefireable; as when you would change the kind of
Fruit on a Stock againft a Wall, the fooner your
End is compaffed, the better.

However if you are forced to practice upon large
Stocks, you muft be content to Graft, becaufe when
the Bark is become thick and ftubborn, it will not
readily part, nor fo handfomely clofe upon the
Bud. But if the Graft happen to mifs (as it will be
very apt to do in large Stocks, if you do not take
care to leave a leading Branch to carry up the Sap
which would otherwife choak the Scion) thofe flen-
der Shoots which fhall be made near the Grafting

place

place, will do right well to inoculate on, sometimes even the same Year.

The Cherry, Plum, and Pear, but especially the latter, if the Stocks be any thing vigorous, almost never fail to answer your Expectations in Budding; and there is one more advantage here, above what can be had in Grafting with respect to the Plum, *viz.* That you may Inoculate pretty surely any Plum on a Damsen, or wild Plum-stock, which yet will be sure to fail you if you Graft on it. But yet this General Rule is always to be regarded with respect not only to this but all other Stocks; that 'tis a vain Expectation to hope for Success if the Sap do not run well, (as we say) that is, if the Bark will not readily be perswaded to part from the Wood of the Stock by the help of the Penknife.

No sort of Fruit is more untoward, and more apt to deceive you in Budding than the Apple, because the Bark is not so ready to part as in other Fruit: Yet I have my self practised it several times with Success on vigorous Shoots put forth near the place where the Graft failed.

Any time between the beginning of *June,* and the latter End of *August,* allowance being made for different seasons, you may Inoculate most Trees; nay I have several times Inoculated Pears in *September* with good Success. But it must be taken notice of, that the Branch or Shoot, which you make choice of for Buds to Inoculate with, must not lye by any time (as in Grafting) but must be immediately made use of, as before directed.

The

The several kinds of Oranges, Lemons, strip'd Philarea's, and Jessamines, are to be propagated by Inoculation. And now I mention the Jessamine, I cannot but take notice to you what a noble Demonstration the yellow strip'd Jessamine has afforded us of the as certain Circulation of the Sap in a Tree, as of the Blood in the Body of an Animal; which matter, altho' it has been believed by some, yet it has been denied by others. And therefore because it has not as yet (as far as I can learn) been brought to any Certainty or Demonstration, I shall here relate the means of this noble Discovery by virtue of Inoculation.

Suppose a plain Jessamine Tree, spreading itself into 2 or 3 Branches from one common Stem near the Root. Into any one of these Branches in *August*, inoculate a Bud, taken from a yellow strip'd Jessamine, where it is to abide all Winter; And in the Summer, when the Tree begins to make its Shoots, you will find here and there some Leaves tinged with Yellow, even on the other Branches not Inoculated, till by degrees in succeeding Years the whole Tree, even the very Wood of all the tender Branches, shall be most beautifully Strip'd and Dy'd with Yellow and Green intermix'd. It is not material whether you cut off the Branch above the Inoculation to make the Bud it self shoot; for it will have the same effect of tinging by degrees all the Sap of the Tree as it passes by or through this Bud, and communicating its Virtue to the most distant and opposite Branches, tho' the Bud it self should not shoot out. Nay I have my self several times experienced,

that

that if the Bud do but live two or three Months and after that happen to die, or be wounded by any Accident, yet even in that little time it will have communicated its Virtue to the whole Sap, and the Tree will become intirely Strip'd. This discovery undoubtedly proves the Circulation of the Sap. *Q. E. D.*

What further Uses and Observations may be made from hence, I leave to other Philosophical Genius's and curious Inquirers into Vegetable Nature; and shall only add to this Chapter, that when you find in the Spring, or the time when the Tree begins to shoot, your Inoculation takes, and the Bud looks green and fresh, you must not forget in all cases (except this of the strip'd Jessamine) to cut off the Head of the Stock slopewise about an Inch above the Bud, the slope ending on that side where the Bud is. It may not be amiss also to add, that where you put in more than one Bud, it is not convenient to place them just one above another, but sideways.

CHAP. VII.

Concerning the proper Disposition of Trees against a Wall; the best kinds of each; their Order and Time of Ripening.

IN speaking to these several Points, there are great Allowances to be made for the great variety and difference of Soil, which as to the ripening and perfecting of Fruit has more in it than most people are aware of. For I question not but a good Soil,

viz.

viz. a rich deep fandy mixt Earth, in fifty four Degrees of Latitude, will do more towards accelerating the ripening the beſt Fruit than a bad one, *viz.* a ſtiff cold Clay will do in fifty one. And ſo a North-weſt Wall in an extraordinary good Soil will do as well for a Buree or a Vine, as a South weſt Wall will do for the ſame in a bad one In equal Degrees of Latitude. The Rules therefore that I ſhould lay down muſt be calculated for the common ſtate and condition of moſt Places in *England,* which generally want all the Advantages that Art can give them to ripen the beſt and lateſt Fruit. Moſt that know any thing of Gardening can tell that a Peach, an Apricot and a Vine are to be ſet againſt their beſt Walls, but as for Figs and Pears, tho' of the beſt *French* ſort, they are ordinarily crowded into any Corner, or againſt a North-Eaſt or North-Weſt Wall; whereas in truth many of them deſerve the very beſt Place in the Garden, eſpecially in ſuch a Garden as lyes upon a moiſt Clay, which yet may be made by the Directions already laid down *Chap.* I. agreeable enough to the beſt Pears, Figs and Plums. And truly thoſe who have the Misfortune of a cold Soil, I cannot but adviſe not to ſtrive too much againſt Nature, in aiming to have the late Frontiniack Grapes, or the choiceſt Peaches, eſpecially if they lye open and unguarded from the cold Winds, their Expectations will be quickly tired with watry unripe Fruit, whereas if they did but ſuit their Soil with proper kinds, they might be rewarded with ſomething good: For I am of Sir *William Temple's* mind, that a good Plum is much better than a bad Peach.   As

As to an exact and proper Catalogue of the best kinds of the several sorts of Fruit, no other can be expected than what the Author most approves of himself, who, in this case, can be supposed to act no otherwise than is common with a Physician as to his general Rules and Directions in Diet for preserving Health, *viz.* to prescribe what he loves himself. If then there is not found in this small Catalogue (suited to the Garden and Persons designed) that particular favourite Sort which some Persons may expect, let it not be concluded that all others but what are here named, are condemned as naught; but rather that it is thought adviseable not to perplex a Lover of Fruit with an unnecessary number and variety of sorts, when he has room only for a few good ones of each kind. He that has room, and would encrease his Collection, may have recourse to *Monsieur Quintinye*, or to the Abridgment by Mr. *London* and *Wise*, and he will quickly have his Curiosity satisfied. In the mean time I shall satisfie my self with such a Collection as seems most proper and suitable to the Garden I am supposing. But before I begin it, I ought to say thus much first, That it must not be thought strange, if sometimes the Fruit here recommended do not answer, but prove watry and insipid, there being a certain agreeableness of Soil peculiar to almost every kind of Fruit; at least thus much is certain, that a good sort of Fruit may prove bad in such a Soil as will make another good sort excellent in it's kind; and the best Peaches may prove bad, where Pears and Apricots will excell; neither ought we too hastily to con-

conclude and give Judgment againſt what may only prove bad from an unkind Seaſon. But when it is found by Experience that the Soil and the kind do not agree, the beſt way is to loſe no more time, but either prepare another for his place, or alter the ſort by Inoculation, which is very eaſie and quickly to be done, if the Stocks be good, and not too big.

The beſt Peaches to be planted againſt a South-Wall, (or inclining to the Eaſt or Weſt) as follow in the Order of their Ripening,

Ripe.

The White Magdalene }
The Minion } Middle of *Auguſt.*

The Right Old *Newington* }
The Chevreux } Beginning of *September.*

The Admirable }
The Nivet } Middle of *September.*

The Red Roman Nectorine, Middle of *September.*

Apricots will do againſt Eaſt and Weſt-Walls.

Ripe,

The Maſculine Apricot,   Middle of *June.*
The Orange Apricot.   Middle of *July.*

Figs muſt be planted againſt a South-Eaſt or South-Weſt Wall. Only two ſorts good.

The White Fig }
The long Purple Fig } End of *Auguſt.*

A Catalogue of the beſt *French* Pears that require the beſt Wall and Aspect you can give them, and will not be ripe till ſome time after they are gathered.

Ripe.

The Summer Bon Crêtien,   Begin. of *Sept.*

The

The Buree du Roy,	End of Sept.
The Verte-Longue,	Octob.
The St. Germain,	Novem.
The Spanish Bon Cretien,	Novem.
The Ambret,	Decem.
Colmat,	Decem.
Chrysan,	Decem.
The Winter Bon Cretien,	March.

Some other good Pears that will do on North-East, or North-West Walls.

The Orange Bergamot	
The St. Katharine	September
The Rousselet	
The Black Pear of *Worcester*	for Baking.
The Pound Pear	

Peculiarly good for Dwarfs.

The Swan's Egg, [*Nulli secundum*]	Octob.
The Bergamot	both well known in *England*.
The Windsor	

The foregoing forts, recommended for North-East, and North-West Walls, will also do well for Dwarfs if occasion be; as there are also many other forts might be added; but needless Varieties I recommend not.

It is very adviseable to plant in such places as are most exposed to Comers and Goers, those kinds of Winter-Pears that are hard and unpalatable, whilst they are on the Tree; otherwise the Owner will reap little else but Disappointment and Vexation. That side of the House, or indeed any of the Out-houses

houses which is exposed to the South, will do singularly well for the Ambret, the St. Germain's, but especially for any of the Bon Cretiens, (except the Summer, which is too tempting) these loving room and height; and as delicious Fruit as they are, will not abide to be tasted a second time when newly taken from the Tree. The Winter Bon-Cretien is remarkable for keeping longest, and all the sorts of them are as remarkable for answering so well the Purport of their Name *Bon Cretien*, or *Good Christian, Sound at Heart* ; (the right sort (alass!) hard to be met with) for as in time they begin to decay and rot in the outward parts or pulp, so it is observed that the Core or Heart continues generally found to the last.

There are several sorts of Grapes, and most of them in some good Years will ripen in *England*; but I think the white Muscadine, and the black Cluster-Grape are the only sorts that one may depend upon to have some pretty good almost any Year. I need not say that all of them expect the best Wall and Aspect we can give them, to help them to that Maturity and dulcedinous Juice which make it either pleasant or safe to eat them in any Quantity. But let the Wall or Aspect be never so good, yet I must repeat it, that if it lye open and exposed without any Break of Hills or Wood at a distance, you will certainly be deceived in your Expectations of good Fruit.

The White Raison-Grape, admirable for Tarts, where there is room enough.

There are also a great Variety of Plums, and
some

some of them so good as to deserve the best Walls, as the blew and white Perdrigons and imperial Plums; but such as follow are those I recommend for Dwarfs. Standards or North East, and North West Walls.

The Orleance,
The Muscle,
The Queen-Mother,   } Plums.
The Damascene,
The Violet,

Fotheringa. Good Bearer, fine Plum.

Perdrigon, blew and White, very good.

Le Royal, the best Plum that grows; but a bad Bearer.

Drop of Gold. A Yellow Russet, good.

The White Bonum Magnum } for Baking.
The Pear Plum

The Damsen every one knows to be good, and it is to be raised from the Stone, or by Suckers without grafting, best a Standard. There are many other good sorts which I mention not, because they are generally idle ill Bearers.

Most Cherries will do on Dwarfs or Standards, but are mended against a Wall: As,

The Orleance or Bloody Heart, } on East or West
The *May*-Duke   } Walls.

The Morella, on a North-wall.

But the Common Flemish is quite spoil'd against a Wall.

It will be necessary before I conclude this Chapter to add, That the time of Fruit's Ripening is very different in different years; and tho' I have fixt

the

the General time, yet it muſt not be wondered at if a bad year make ſome Fruit, eſpecially Winter-Pears, a Month or two later before they come to their Maturity; only I have obſerved when they much exceed their uſual time of ripening, they are never ſo good, and have not their true rich Taſt.

N. B. When it is adviſed here to plant ſuch a Tree againſt a South-Wall, if that Wall happen to decline ſome few Degrees to the Eaſt or Weſt it is never the worſe, but altogether as good, provided the Declination be not above fifteen or twenty Degrees, becauſe in that caſe the Wall would enjoy the ſame Time, and as many Hours of Sun-ſhine: But when I ſay an Eaſt and Weſt Wall will do for an Apricot, 'tis ſuppoſed that there is not the leaſt Declination towards the North; for that would wholly defeat the Deſign, and Expectation of the Planter; ſo that if it have any Declination, it were to be wiſh'd it had it toward the South.

N. B. An Eaſt Aſpect is better for all ſorts of Fruit than a Weſt; not that it can be ſuppoſed to have more Hours of Sun ſhine; but becauſe the early Rays of the Sun take off thoſe cold Dews which are apt to fall and hang upon Fruit in the Night, which in the caſe of a Weſt Wall are not taken off till later in the Day, and conſequently the Fruit is more ſubject to be chill'd. Whether this will be thought a good Reaſon or the only Reaſon I cannot tell; but thus much is certain in experience, that an Eaſt-Wall is better and kinder for all Fruit than a Weſt; and I cannot eaſily be brought to believe that there are any peculiar inherent Virtues and Qualities in the Eastern Rays of the Sun that should cause this Difference in Vegetation.

N. B. I have said nothing about the Management and Culture of Rasberrys, Strawberrys, Goosberrys and Currants, because little skill is required, besides this one Rule, that they are not to stand too long in a place, nor above four or five Years before they be renewed, especially Strawberrys, which must be kept clear from Runners all the time of their Bearing.

N. B. It is of very mischievous, if not dangerous, consequence, to let Rosemary grow too near any of your Fruit-trees, especially if they be young; for that will not fail to rob them of so much of their proper Nourishment, as that they will be infallibly weakned, if not in danger of being kill'd.

The CONCLUSION.

I Have now gone over some of the most considerable Particulars relating to the Art of Gardening, and (I hope) not *mal à-propos.* Thus much at least I have endeavoured, to speak intelligibly, to lay down my Rules and Observations in a tolerable Method, and to avoid unnecessary Prolixity. All which I have constantly had in my Eye, that I might in some degree attain the End I aim at, *viz.* To make those Persons (especially those of my own Order) who may not have had so much Experience in this particular Science, in love with so innocent, so agreeable and so profitable a Diversion.

I might have added, as some others have done, a Chapter about the several Diseases which the different Sorts of Trees are subject to; but except a proper Remedy were also added, it is to little purpose to

men-

mention the Disease: and as far as my Observation
has gone, I plainly perceive most are incurable, and
therefore have always chose to have recourse to my
Nursery for another to put in the Place. The
Gum and Canker are plainly incurable, and the part
affected must be cut off, except there remain a sound
part sufficient to convey the Sap: Wet cold Soils
are most subject to these, and therefore in such case,
the best preventing Physick you can give is to plant
high. Moss should be carefully rubb'd off with the
Back of a Knife or piece of Hair-Cloath after a
Shower of Rain.

Because both Grass and Gravel Walks are so much
the Ornament and Beauty of a Garden, and do afford
so considerable a Pleasure to a thoughtful contemplative Person, I cannot but here insert a speedy e-
ffectual Method of destroying Worms, those filthy
Annoyers and Spoilers of the Beauty of all Walks.

Any time in Autumn fill a Cistern, or any large
Trough with Water, putting thereinto a large Quantity of Walnut Leaves; where let them steep at least
a Fortnight or Three Weeks: in which time the
Water will have received such a Bitterness, that if
you pour gently a small Quantity of it on such Places as are most annoyed with Worms, by that time
the Water can be supposed to reach them, you will
find the Worms hurrying in great Confusion out of
their Holes, so as to crawl in great Plenty under
your Feet upon the Ground, where they may be gathered up and thrown away. They may indeed be
taken by a Candle and Lanthorn in a Summer's Evening after Rain; but this may be practised any time
in the Day with Pleasure, and it will certainly destroy

ſtroy them, if it be but carefully practiſed and repeated: Only be ſure to put Walnut Leaves enough that the Water be very bitter, otherwiſe it will do no good.

It is very convenient to have ſuch a large Ciſtern or Stone Trough as I here ſpeak of, as for the aforegoing Uſe, ſo alſo for a Treaſury of Rain Water, wherewith to refreſh your Flowers and new planted Trees in the Droughts of *April* and *June*. And for this Reaſon it ſhould be fix'd under ſuch Parts of the Houſe where the greateſt Plenty of Rain-Water is made to deſcend, where alſo it will be found to be not a little ſerviceable to the Family in the Winter. And if it ſhall be thought difficult (as indeed it is) to procure ſuch a ſort of Stone as will endure the hard Froſts in the Winter; as a Remedy for this, I my ſelf made an Experiment upon a very brittle Stone Trough, which the Maſon himſelf told me would not endure the Froſt, and it ſucceeded according to my Expectations. I uſed it for ſalting Meat in the Houſe, for two or three Months, till I thought it was throughly ſoak'd with Brine, and then ſet it abroad, and it has already endured ſix Winters, and defied even the great Froſts in 1708.

N. B. I have ſaid nothing concerning Apples, becauſe they are generally Standards, and require little Art to manage them, and if they are Dwarfs, muſt be ordered as Pears. It would be endleſs to mention the beſt Kinds; For thoſe are the Beſt, that are beſt and moſt proſperous in that particular Soyl and Place: each Country having commonly its known and peculiar ſort of Apple, which they call Beſt, which would not, it may be, prove beſt in another.

F I N I S.

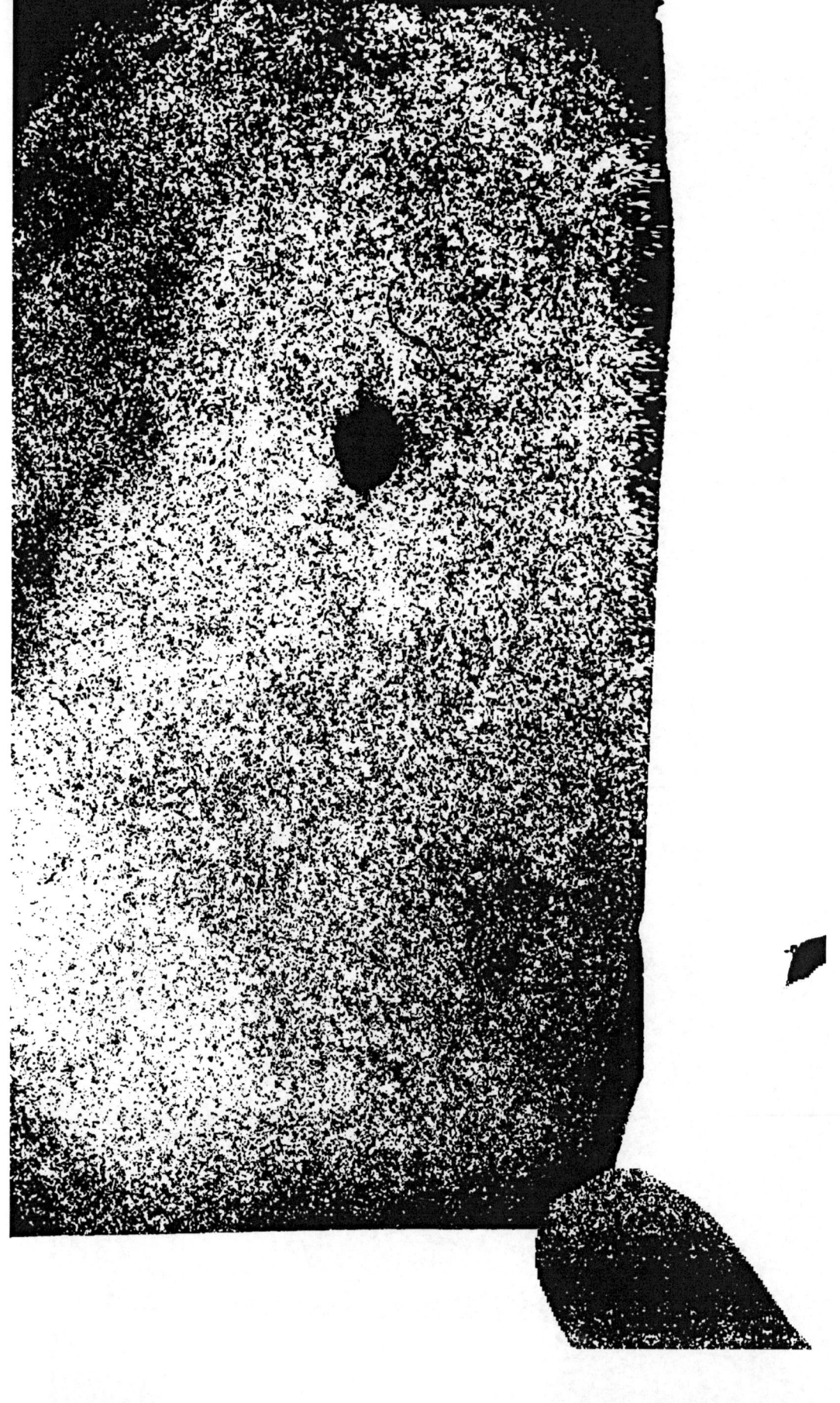

Lightning Source UK Ltd.
Milton Keynes UK
02 September 2010

159341UK00005B/24/P